GREAT PETS

Turtles

Johannah Haney

 **Marshall Cavendish**
Benchmark
New York

With thanks to Scott R. Miner, DVM, for his expert review of the manuscript.

Marshall Cavendish Benchmark
99 White Plains Road
Tarrytown, New York 10591-9001
www.marshallcavendish.us

All Web sites were available and accurate when this book was sent to press.

Library of Congress Cataloging-in-Publication Data
Haney, Johannah.
Turtles / by Johannah Haney.
p. cm. — (Great pets)
Summary: "Describes the characteristics and behavior of pet turtles,
also discussing the physical appearance and place in the history of turtles"—Provided by publisher.
Includes bibliographical references and index.
ISBN 978-0-7614-2709-4
1. Turtles as pets—Juvenile literature. I. Title.

SF459.T8H345 2007
639.3'92—dc22
2006038157

Front cover: A Western box turtle
Back cover: A cooter turtle
Photo Research by Candlepants Incorporated
The photographs in this book are used by permission and through the courtesy of:
Photo Researchers Inc.: Tom McHugh, 4; Williams H. Mullins, 18; Jeffrey Greenberg, 19. *The Bridgeman Art Library:* Boltin
Picture Library, 6. *Corbis:* Blue Lantern Studio, 7; Christian Simonpietri/Sygma, 8; Stephen Frink, 16; Joe McDonald, 29,
39; Lynda Richardson, 30. *SuperStock:* Brand X, 9. *Peter Arnold Inc.:* BIOS Cavignaux Régis, 10; R. Andrew Odum, 25; Ed
Reschke, 37; PHONE Labat J.M. / Rocher P., 22. *Animals Animals:* Joe McDonald, 1, 23, 42; Doug Wechsler, 13; Robert
Lubeck, 14; Breck P. Kent, 20; Gerard Lacz, 21, 33: Maresa Pryor, 24, 32, back cover. *Renee Stockdale:* 26, 35.

Editor: Karen Ang
Publisher: Michelle Bisson
Art Director: Anahid Hamparian
Series Designer: Elynn Cohen

Printed in Malaysia
3 5 6 4 2

Contents

Chapter 1	**A World of Turtles**	5
Chapter 2	**Choosing Your Pet Turtle**	11
Chapter 3	**Types of Turtles**	17
Chapter 4	**Caring For Your Turtle**	27
Glossary		44
Find Out More		46
Index		48

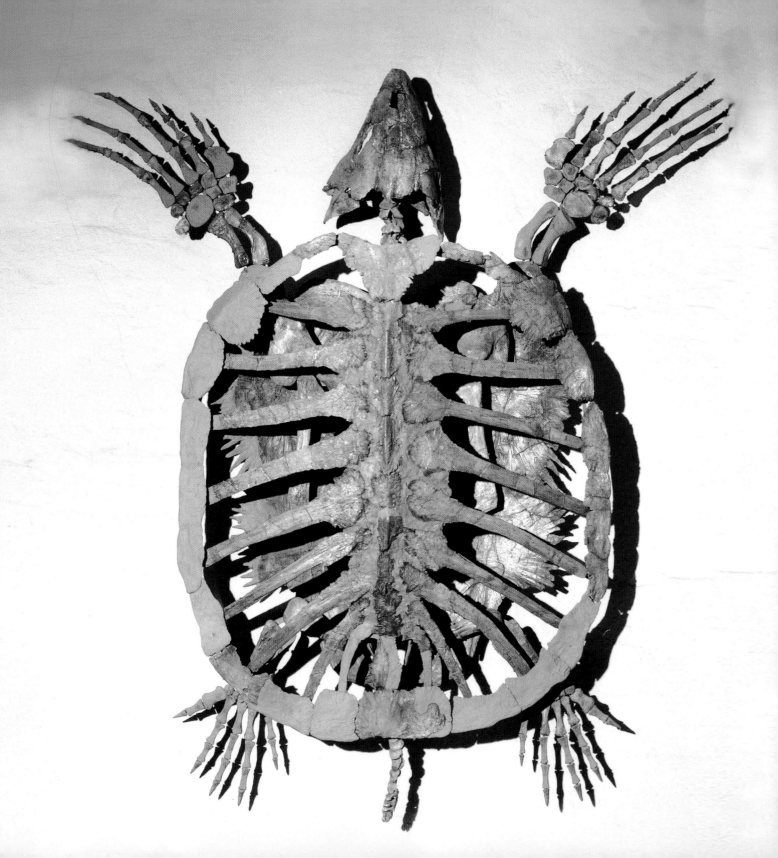

1

A World of Turtles

People have long been fascinated by the slow pace of land turtles, the majesty of sea turtles, and the unique homes turtles carry right on their backs. If you have ever admired the turtle's slow but steady crawl or marveled at its abilities to protect itself, a turtle might be the perfect pet for you.

History and Mythology

Turtles and their ancestors have been swimming the sea and walking across the land for more than 200 million years. Over time, they have evolved—or changed—to adapt to the environment. But the modern turtle's ancestors were swimming and walking next to the dinosaurs!

More than 100 million years ago, parts of North America were completely covered by an inland sea. This skeleton is from a turtle that swam in those prehistoric waters. Scientists think that some of these turtles were 10 feet long.

This Mayan statue shows a man—possibly a god—standing on a turtle's back. The ancient Maya believed that Earth was on the back of a giant turtle or crocodile floating in the sea.

Throughout their long history, turtles have been very important to humans. In many cultures, turtles are mystical creatures that bear the weight of the world on their backs. According to the myths of the Hindu religion—which is practiced mostly in India—the world is supported by four elephants standing on the shell of a giant turtle.

Some groups of Native Americans tell a traditional story in which Earth was completely underwater until a giant turtle shell rose from the water. The shell created land upon which people and animals could live. The Iroquois Native Americans have a myth in which a woman fell from a world in the sky and landed on the back of a turtle. Soil then spread over the turtle's shell and became

The Island of the Turtle's Back. Many Native American groups believed the souls of their ancestors lived on in turtles, so they lovingly cared for these creatures.

Chinese legends say that the patterns on the turtle's shell form a map that shows the best places to grow plants for food. Turtles can live for a very long time—some more than 200 years! This makes them a symbol for good health and long life in many cultures.

Turtles and tortoises show up in many stories and books. In Aesop's fable, *The Tortoise and the Hare,* a confident rabbit cannot imagine that a slow turtle could beat him in a race. The rabbit is so sure that he takes a nap during the race, while the turtle keeps

Throughout the years, the fable about the tortoise and the hare has been illustrated in many books and paintings.

going at a slow and steady pace. Imagine the rabbit's surprise when he wakes up to find the turtle beat him across the finish line! The turtle shows us that persistence and determination lead to success.

TURTLE, TORTOISE, OR TERRAPIN?

People around the world have different ways of referring to the **reptiles** we call turtles. Some countries call them "terrapins," which comes from the Algonquian Native Americans. Many scientists call turtles and tortoises by their scientific name, chelonians. Most people in the United States use the word turtles to refer to all four-legged reptiles with a shell. (In this book, all pet turtles, tortoises, and terrapins are called "turtles.") But here is the scientific difference between each of these names:

• A turtle spends most of its life in the sea or in the water.

• A tortoise spends most of its life on land.

• A terrapin spends its life both on land and in fresh water.

Turtles have also helped to shape parts of modern-day culture. Movie producer and director Steven Spielberg used the faces of Galapagos tortoises as the inspiration for his beloved—and world-famous—character, ET.

Some of ET's features closely resemble a turtle with its head sticking out of its shell.

Is a Turtle Right for You?

Like all pets, keeping a healthy turtle requires hard work, patience, and time. You will need to provide the proper food and a safe living environment. It is also important to remember that turtles can live a long time. So when you get a pet turtle you are making a big commitment. But that also means you can enjoy many years of turtle companionship.

One of the world's oldest tortoises, Harriet, died in 2006 at the Australia Zoo. She lived to be 176 years old. But Harriet was not the oldest tortoise on record. A tortoise named Tui Malila lived to be 188!

With some hard work and a lot of affection, turtles can make perfect pets.

2

Choosing Your Pet Turtle

Many pet shops carry turtles that are just waiting for homes. In many towns there are also turtle and tortoise clubs. These are groups that breed and raise turtles. The people who belong to these clubs can help you find the turtle that is perfect for you.

The best type of turtle to buy or adopt is one that has been hatched in **captivity**. This means that the eggs came from turtles who were being cared for in human homes. Most turtles hatched in captivity are healthy. Many turtle and tortoise clubs sell turtles that have been raised in captivity. These clubs also look for homes for abandoned pet turtles. You can also ask a local **veterinarian** (also called a vet) for suggestions about where to find a good pet turtle.

Owning a young turtle can be very fun, but your new pet should not be too young. Good pet stores and trustworthy turtle breeders will never sell you a baby turtle that is less than 4 inches long.

It is against the law in the United States to sell a turtle that is less than 4 inches long. Some states require special permits to keep any turtles as pets. Indiana, Maryland, New Jersey, New York, Ohio, and Virginia all have special requirements for turtle owners. Check the laws in your state by calling a local veterinarian, your local Humane Society, or the state's Department of Fish and Wildlife before you get your new pet turtle.

Places to Avoid

Sometimes you can find people selling turtles at flea markets, fairs, or carnivals. Veterinarians and experienced turtle owners will tell you these are not the best places to buy your pet turtle. Many of these turtles were taken from their natural habitat and are unlikely to live long as pets. Also, it might be against the law to own some of these turtles. Some states have laws against keeping certain turtles as pets.

If you get a turtle that was born in the wild, the turtle will most likely be sick when you buy it. Moving from a wild habitat to a captive environment is very stressful for turtles. Many of these turtles will have tiny organisms living inside of them. These **parasites** can make turtles—and even humans—very sick.

You might see a turtle in the road, in the woods near your house, or at a local pond or lake. Some people decide to take these turtles home to raise as pets. However, this is not a good idea. These are wild animals and should remain in the wild. It is difficult to know what type of turtle you are taking, so it is impossible to know the right way to take care of it. For example, the

On a sunny day, you may see many wild turtles—like these Diamondback Terrapins—basking in the sun. As pretty as these turtles are, they are wild animals and should not be brought home as pets.

turtle you see on the road might be little, but it may grow to be too large to keep in your home. Other types of turtles are endangered **species**. This means there are not very many of those turtles left in the wild. Endangered turtles should be left in the wild so they can be with other turtles and continue the growth of the species.

Like all turtles, snapping turtles are very small when they are young. Certain types of snappers can grow to weigh at least 40 pounds.

How to Pick a Healthy Turtle

No matter where you buy or adopt your turtle, make sure the people have been taking good care of their turtles. If it seems like there are too many turtles in one tank, or the tank is dirty or smells bad, then the turtles kept there will most likely be sick.

When you look for a healthy turtle you should check for the following things:

- It should have clear and alert eyes.
- Its shell should look whole and be free of cracks.
- The skin on its head and legs should be clean and unbroken.
- A turtle's nose and mouth should look clean and free of swelling.

Do not be afraid to ask questions. You can ask how long the pet store or turtle breeders have been handling and selling turtles. Be sure to ask about the type of turtle you are bringing home. How big will the turtle get? How often does the turtle eat and what should you feed it? What kind of habitat should you set up for the turtle? Getting these answers will provide you with information you need to care for your new pet. It will also tell you whether or not you can trust the people from whom you are buying the turtle. People who can easily answer these questions will most likely be selling or giving you a healthy turtle.

3

Types of Turtles

Today, many species—or types—of turtles are endangered. One reason is because turtle parts have long been used to make different products. Throughout history, turtles have been hunted for their beautifully-patterned shells. In the 1800s, jewelry made from tortoise shells was very popular. In many places turtles are used for food. More recently, pollution, fishing, hunting, and habitat disruption have threatened some types of turtles. Organizations like the World Wildlife Fund, turtle and tortoise clubs, and other nature preservation societies are working to protect endangered turtles.

By Land and by Sea

If you go to a zoo or aquarium, or go snorkeling in the ocean, you might see large sea turtles swimming quickly through the water. Many sea turtles

Green sea turtles should never be kept as pets. They are an endangered species, and in the wild they swim through warm oceans and salty seas.

All turtles are **cold-blooded.** This means that they cannot control their body temperatures on their own. They must rely on their environment to stay warm or cool. Turtles need the rays of the Sun to keep warm. They move into shade or colder water to cool down.

In the wild, many turtles will hide in burrows to get some shade from the hot sun.

live in shallow, warm waters near the coast. Unlike land turtles, sea turtles have flippers that allow them to swim. Some turtles can swim as fast as 40 miles per hour. Sea turtles in the wild can grow to be more than 4 feet long and weigh more than 400 pounds. These types of turtles, however, are not the kind that you would take home as a pet.

The most common types of water turtle people keep as pets are red-eared sliders, cooters, and painted turtles. They can each grow to be 10 to 12 inches long. These turtles spend part of the time swimming and part of the time basking in the sun.

Turtles that live mainly on land are sometimes called tortoises. Although they live on land, tortoises need to have water for soaking and for drinking. Soaking their bodies helps the tortoise keep its skin and shell healthy. The Galapagos tortoise is one of the most famous land turtles. These large reptiles can be found in zoos around the world, but their natural habitat is on the Galapagos Islands, which are located in the Pacific

Visitors to the Galapagos Islands can see the giant tortoises in their natural habitat.

Ocean off the coast of South America. Galapagos tortoises can weigh up to 600 pounds and live for more than 150 years. But these large tortoises are not household pets. The box turtle is one of the most popular land turtles kept as a pet.

Turtle Varieties

There are many different types of turtles that can be kept as pets. Some need dry habitats, while others should be kept in habitats that are mostly filled with water. Certain types of turtles are harder to find in stores, and some require more care than others. You should research the different types of pet turtles available before choosing one.

Box Turtles

A box turtle is an **omnivore**, which means it eats both plants and meat. (**Herbivores** eat only plants and **carnivores** eat only meat.) They live on land, and in the wild they usually **hibernate** in the winter. Fully grown box turtles grow to be 6 to 7 inches in length and weigh just less than a pound.

Box turtles are happiest in an outdoor pen with some sun exposure and some shade. They need enough dirt to

With their brightly patterned shells, Eastern box turtles are very popular pets.

make a cozy hole where they can hide and rest. Box turtles must also have enough water for drinking and soaking.

If a box turtle is kept indoors, it needs a large **terrarium** with fresh water, an area with soil for burrowing, and a bottom lined with newspaper or artificial grass. It can be difficult to maintain the best conditions for a box turtle indoors, but a local turtle and tortoise club can offer tips on making your turtle comfortable.

Red-Eared Sliders

Spending part of its life in water and part of its life basking in the Sun on land, a red-eared slider is a wonderful type of turtle to keep as a pet. Young red-eared sliders eat a mix of meat and plants, including worms, minnows (small fish), lettuce, and fruit. As they get older, the turtles start to prefer a vegetarian diet. Red-eared sliders can grow up to 1 foot long.

Red-eared sliders get their name from the stripes of red on the sides of their heads.

A mud turtle pauses to rest in its outdoor habitat.

Mud and Musk Turtles

Mud and musk turtles are actually different species, but they are so closely related that the care for these two types of turtle is basically the same. Mud and musk turtles thrive in a damp, sandy, or muddy home. They are omnivorous and will eat plants and small insects or worms. Both mud turtles and musk turtles give off a foul smell when they feel scared or are in danger. But many mud and musk turtles raised in captivity never find a reason to release their offensive smell.

Mud turtles can grow to be 3 to 5 inches long. They are a little smaller than other types of turtles, which makes them excellent pets.

Painted Turtles

Bright stripes of red and yellow skin mark the neck and legs of these beautiful turtles. Some species also have red spots on their shells. Painted turtles spend a lot of time in the water, but also need dry land for basking

Many turtle breeders raise painted turtles to be sold or adopted as pets.

in sunlight. They enjoy sleeping on a log or rock so they can be partially submerged in water. Painted turtles eat small fish, insects, and plants. These turtles can grow to be about 4 to 10 inches long.

Cooters

Cooters are aquatic turtles that can sometimes grow to be longer than 12 inches. In their natural habitat, they live in rivers, lakes, or ponds, so they should have access to plenty of water for swimming. They also require a sunny spot for basking when the water is cold. Cooters eat a mix of water plants, insects, and small fish.

A young cooter dives down to the bottom of its aquarium to get some food.

Spotted Turtle

Spotted turtles are mainly black in color, but they have yellow spots on their head, neck, legs, and shell. These turtles can grow to be 5 inches long, and mainly eat meat.

The number of spotted turtles in nature is decreasing. This is because the land where they live is being developed for buildings, and so many spotted turtles have been collected from the wild as pets. If you want a spotted turtle as a pet, make sure you buy one that has been hatched in captivity.

MALE OR FEMALE?

Some pet owners often wonder if it is better to have a male or female turtle as a pet. Most experts agree that either males or females can make great pets. If you are still curious, a veterinarian can examine your turtle.

After a long swim, this spotted turtle rests on a piece of wood in its terrarium.

25

4

Caring for
Your Turtle

Turtle Bodies

Before bringing home your new turtle, it is important to know a little bit about its body. What are its different parts? What role do they play in keeping the turtle happy and healthy? Do turtles require special care because of these features?

The Shell

The most noticeable part of a turtle is its shell. The shell grows as the turtle grows. A turtle's upper shell—the rounded part that is on its "back"—is called the **carapace**. On many turtles, the carapace is covered by scales or plates called **scutes.** The different scutes fit together like puzzle pieces.

Most turtles need water to keep their skin and shell healthy.

TURTLE SKELETON

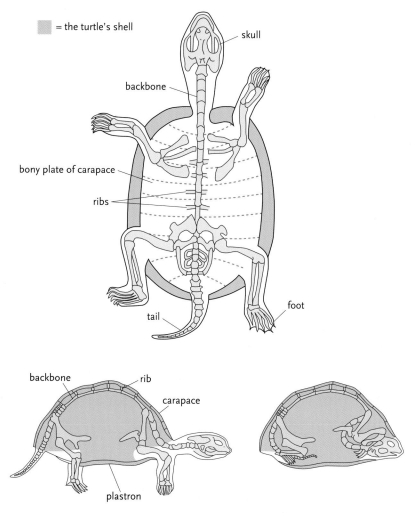

= the turtle's shell

skull

backbone

bony plate of carapace

ribs

tail

foot

backbone

rib

carapace

plastron

This illustration shows the different parts of a turtle's skeleton and how it can withdraw into its shell.

Some turtles' scutes have interesting rings and patterns.

When they feel threatened, many types of turtles can withdraw their legs and head into the carapace. Other types of turtles fold their necks to the side to hide from danger. Some turtles, such as the African pancake tortoise, have a soft and flexible carapace that allows them to easily hide between rocks.

The **plastron** is the turtle's bottom shell. This is the part that would be on its "belly." The plastron is connected to the carapace by bony bridges. These bridges protect the turtle by making it nearly impossible to separate the turtle from its carapace.

Although many turtles' shells are hard and tough, remember that it is an important part of the turtle and it can be damaged. You should never knock on a turtle's shell. Owners must also be careful that the turtle does not fall on its shell. A cracked or broken shell is very painful for a turtle. A cracked shell can also make a turtle sick. If your turtle has a crack or break in its shell, take your pet to a veterinarian. He or she can properly repair it.

Some turtles have colorfully patterned shells, while others do not. Never use paint or other chemicals to make patterns on your turtle's shell. You should also avoid taping or gluing anything to the shells. A turtle's shell needs air to stay healthy. Paint or other materials block the air and can make the turtle sick.

This Eastern box turtle withdraws into its shell because it is feeling threatened.

The Head

Instead of teeth, turtles have a beak. This beak is made of very tough hornlike material that makes it possible to break through tough pieces of meat or sturdy plants. Turtles that eat a lot of plants have ridges on their beaks to help them bite off chewy plant material. Some turtles, such as snapping turtles, have jaws strong and sharp enough to bite off a finger!

Turtles have pretty good eyesight. Their eyes, however, are soft and can be damaged easily. Turtles have eyelids that they can close to protect their eyes. When handling your turtle or setting up its habitat, be sure that there

For most turtles, the nose is basically two small nostrils at the tip of the face.

are no sharp objects or corners that can hurt it. Turtles' eyes can become infected if their homes are very dirty, so it is important to provide your turtle with a clean habitat.

Though their sense of smell is good, most turtles do not have noses that stick out of their faces. Usually, turtles have two holes or **nostrils** at the end of their heads. Like most animals, the turtle breathes when air moves in and out of the nostrils. To stay underwater, many turtles hold their breath for a very long time. However, some water turtles can take in oxygen through their skin, allowing them to breathe underwater for long periods of time.

Turtles do not have ears that stick out of their heads. But they do have parts inside their head specially designed to hear sounds and sense vibrations. Most turtles cannot hear sounds in the air as well as you can, but they can be very sensitive to vibrations—especially in the water.

The Legs

All turtles have four legs covered in scaly skin. Depending upon the type of turtle, the legs end in flippers or with claws. Some turtles have three toes on each leg, while others have five. A turtle uses its claws to help it move around and to dig up food or a hole to rest in. Some turtle claws can be very sharp, so you must be careful when handling your pet. In most cases, you never have to trim your turtle's claws. When turtle nails grow too long—which is not often—it is best to have your veterinarian check and trim them.

Turtle Habitats

Turtles can be kept indoors or outdoors. An outdoor turtle needs to live in a fenced-in area or a space with sturdy walls. This will prevent the turtle from wandering off. It also protects your pet from outdoor animals such as neighborhood dogs, raccoons, or skunks. Make sure the turtle's outdoor home is also protected from bad weather.

Your turtle needs a lot of sunlight, but it should have a shady area where it can cool off. It is very important that your turtle has water at all times

Some people put grass or moss in their turtle's outdoor habitat.

so it can drink and bathe. Unless your turtle is a water turtle that swims well, the water in your turtle's outdoor home should be shallow. If a turtle is in water that is too deep, it can grow too tired to keep swimming and it will drown. For a land turtle habitat, at its deepest point the water level should reach just below the turtle's chin. The area with water should slope up gradually toward the dry land area. To keep the water clean, many turtle owners set up underwater filtration systems. These can be purchased at pet stores.

Make sure there is nothing in your turtle's water that could trap it underwater, such as certain parts of a filtration system, decorative rocks, or plants. If your water turtle is indoors, you can follow those same instructions in its indoor home.

If you keep your turtle indoors, make sure it has enough space to have a water area, a land area, and a dry space where it can hide when it wants to. This hiding place

A red-eared slider swims to the top of his tank to take a breath.

can be a wooden box or a hollow artificial log made of plastic. Plastic or wooden logs or caves are sold at most pet stores. Many people use a glass aquarium as a home for their indoor turtle. Pet stores also sell sturdy, clear plastic containers for pets like turtles. An aquarium or plastic container for a full-grown turtle needs to be large enough so that it has room to swim, bask, and hide. For example, a 10-inch-long red-eared slider would need at least a 60-gallon aquarium. (Aquariums are measured according to how many gallons of water they can hold.) If you get a baby turtle it might seem small at first, but some types of turtles can grow fast. So you will need to get a bigger terrarium as your turtle grows.

How much water you have in your indoor habitat depends on your turtle. Water turtles will need aquariums that are mostly filled with water. However, these tanks should still have a dry place where your turtle can rest out of the water. You can provide that by having a pile of rocks—real or artificial—that stick out of the water. Make sure your turtle can easily climb onto these rocks. Land turtles do not need as much water. As in an outdoor habitat, you can have shallow water sloping up toward the dry area. Some turtle owners keep a large but shallow water dish inside the terrarium. Your land turtle should be able to climb into and out of the dish whenever it wants.

Indoor turtles need a lot of light. Indoor turtles may not get a lot of natural sunlight, so you will need to provide it with a special ultraviolet (UV) light. There are two types of ultraviolet light bulbs—UVA and UVB. Use the UVB lights for your turtle. Besides the UVB light, your turtle might

All parts of a turtle's terrarium should be cleaned regularly—even its hiding place.

also need a heat lamp. These lamps provide light, but more importantly, they provide the heat that the turtle needs to keep its body going. A veterinarian or a turtle breeder can advise you on the type of heat lamp you should purchase and how you should use it. You need an adult's help in setting up the heat lamp, since a very hot lamp may become a dangerous fire hazard.

Keeping Them Clean

Turtles' living environments need to be kept very clean. Dirty water can cause eye or skin infections. It also smells bad and can be harmful to you and your pet. Remove your turtle's droppings from its aquarium every day. Replace the turtle's water every day. If you have a water filter set up, clean the filter every week. A veterinarian can give you good advice about cleaning the turtle's water.

Once a week, move your turtle to a temporary home (a shoebox with some newspaper on the bottom would be very comfortable for your turtle) so you can thoroughly scrub the tank and everything inside of it. You should wash everything either in a tub or outside. Never wash your turtle's habitat in a kitchen or bathroom sink.

Do not use soap to clean your turtle's home. Most soaps do not rinse off easily and this can poison your turtle. Usually, very hot water will clean up most messes. If the turtle habitat is very dirty or needs a thorough cleaning, you can have an adult use water with a little bit of bleach. Bleach is a very dangerous chemical and it can be harmful to both humans and pets, so it should only be handled by adults. A veterinarian or a local pet store can advise you on how to make the proper bleach solution. The tank and every-thing inside must be rinsed very well in order to protect your turtle.

Turtles do not need much grooming help from their humans. Every so often, turtles will shed their skin, which is called **molting.** Unlike a snake that molts all at once, a turtle will molt a little bit at a time. The molting skin will look like whitish flakes on your turtle's head or legs. Never pull on this skin. In time it will come off on its own.

Feeding Your Turtle

Turtles need a variety of foods to stay healthy. Most turtles like fruits, such as apples and berries. Lettuce, carrots, and tomatoes are also good for the turtles. If your turtle eats meat as well as vegetables, you should feed it small

Fresh fruits and vegetables should be a major part of your turtle's diet.

fish (if it is a water turtle), worms, crickets or certain types of canned cat food. Worms and crickets that are specifically used as pet food can be bought from pet stores.

Unlike pets such as cats and dogs, turtles do not need to be fed every day. Most turtles should be fed two to three times per week. You should check with your veterinarian about how much and how often you should feed your turtle. Overfeeding your pet can make it sick and can make its habitat very dirty.

It is important to give your turtle something hard to eat regularly. This helps keep the turtle's beak short. If a turtle is given soft foods all the time, the beak can grow too long, and it must be trimmed or filed down by a vet.

The best way to give a turtle its food is to place the food on a small plate or dish in its habitat. Most turtles do not like to eat from your hand. In fact, it can be dangerous to try to feed your turtle by hand. Its beak is very sharp and strong, and can injure your fingers. If your turtle is a picky eater, try mixing its favorite foods with other nutritious foods so it can get a little of everything in each bite. When your turtle is finished eating, remove the uneaten food. This will help keep its home clean.

A turtle needs certain vitamins and minerals to keep its shell healthy. Calcium will keep the carapace strong. There are several types of powders—called calcium supplements—that can be added to their food. Eggshells and cuttlefish bone are also good sources of calcium for your turtle. Turtles also need vitamin D to keep their shells healthy. Outdoors, turtles get their vitamin D through the Sun's rays. Indoor turtles should be allowed to bask in natural light as often as possible. Special UVB lights should also be used indoors to give the turtle the amount of vitamin D that it needs to stay healthy.

Veterinary Care

Just like cats, dogs, and other pets, turtles will need care from a veterinarian. However, not all vets treat turtles. Ask your local turtle and tortoise club or pet shop about vets who treat pet turtles in your area. You can also contact the Association of Reptilian and Amphibian Veterinarians to ask for a vet who treats turtles in your area. When you first bring home your pet turtle, you should make an appointment to have it checked out by your vet. The vet can give you good advice on how to take care of your pet.

Certain diseases and conditions are common for turtles, and require the attention of a vet. Many turtles get infected with parasites. Your vet can check your turtle for parasites and give you instructions—and possibly medication—to help get rid of the parasites.

Other reasons a turtle might need to go to a vet include infections similar to a cold, infected bumps or lumps on the skin, broken or infected shells, or overgrown beaks or claws.

Check your turtle regularly to make sure that its shell is not cracked and that its skin is not torn or cut. Do not forget to check its plastron.

Bring your turtle to the vet right away if you notice:

- Any kind of injury
- A cracked or broken shell
- Soft spots on the shell
- Swollen eyes
- Bubbles or crusty material in the nostrils
- A lump on the skin
- Uneven shell growth
- Lack of appetite or no appetite
- Weight loss

Hibernation

Many types of turtles hibernate in the winter, including several types of box turtles. Hibernation occurs in nature when the weather is cold and food is hard to find. A turtle will dig a hole in the ground and crawl inside to "sleep" until spring. The turtle's heart and breathing slow down, and it lives on body fat that it built up during the warm months. Some species of turtle that live outdoors will hibernate as the weather gets cooler and the days get shorter. Signs your turtle is starting to hibernate include decreased activity or moving very slowly, a lack of **appetite**, or spending most of its time in a dark corner or hole. You should call your veterinarian and describe how your turtle is acting. The vet might ask to see the turtle or will give you instructions on how to care for your pet as it prepares to hibernate.

Hibernation is a natural process, so your turtle should know what to do.

Turtles that live outside will dig a hole in the ground in which to hibernate. Make sure the turtle chooses a spot that is not likely to flood. Your turtle will reemerge when the weather starts to warm up. Make sure you give it plenty of food and fresh water when it awakens from hibernation.

Some turtle owners will provide hibernating conditions for their indoor turtles. It can be tricky to safely hibernate an indoor turtle, so ask your vet how to hibernate an indoor turtle if you choose to do so. But keep in mind that it is not necessary for indoor turtles to hibernate since it will have access to food and warmth throughout the cold months.

Handling Your Turtle

Unlike cats, dogs, birds, and many other household pets, most turtles do not like being picked up or handled a lot. But there will be times when you need to pick up your turtle to make sure it is healthy or to clean its aquarium. You should never handle your turtle without an adult helping or watching you. This can prevent you or your turtle from getting hurt.

Always pick up your turtle with two hands, one hand on either side of the shell. Keep your hands and fingers far enough away from its mouth. Never pick up a turtle by its tail. This can cause the turtle a lot of pain. To turn the turtle over to look at its plastron, slowly rotate it head over tail instead of side to side. When you are turning over the turtle, the organs inside its body—like the heart and stomach—move around. Moving slowly allows the organs to adjust to the changing position. Turning your turtle over too quickly can cause it a lot of harm. When you are done looking at

Learning to hold your turtle the right way can prevent injuries to you and your pet.

its plastron, turn your turtle right side up again by moving in the same direction—head-over-tail—instead of changing directions. Gently put your turtle back on stable ground and leave it alone so that it can calm down and become comfortable again.

Turtle Safety

Your pet turtle needs to be kept safe from certain dangers. Many larger animals—indoors and outdoors—may view your pet turtle as their next meal. Turtle habitats should be secure so that other animals cannot open them up or knock them over. If you have your turtle out of its habitat, be sure to keep your dog or cat away. They may look like they want to play with your turtle, but it can be dangerous for all of your pets.

Certain plants are poisonous to turtles. Daffodils, sweet pea, poinsettia, ivy, and buttercups are among the plants you should keep away from your turtle. Turtles are especially attracted to brightly colored fruits and plants. But they do not always know the difference between a bright red strawberry and a small, bright red plastic or metal toy. The strawberry would make a great meal, but trying to eat the toy could seriously hurt your turtle. Keep small things your turtle could swallow out of reach. If you think your turtle swallowed something it should not have, take it to the vet right away.

Since turtles have been walking on land and swimming in the sea for so long, some people think of them as living fossils. And having a "pet fossil" is pretty neat. Keeping a turtle as a pet is a lot of work and an important commitment. But the time and effort you put into caring for your pet is worth it. You get the joys of watching your fascinating reptilian friend grow and thrive.

HUMAN SAFETY

Certain turtles carry a type of **bacteria**—or germ—called *Salmonella* on their skin and shells. This is normal for turtles and does not harm them in any way. But if you pick up a turtle and then touch your face, you could become very sick. To prevent *Salmonella* infections from your pet turtle, never kiss your turtle. Make sure to always wash your hands with antibacterial soap after you handle your turtle or touch anything in its habitat. If you use a bathtub to clean your turtle's habitat, have an adult help you scrub the tub with a strong detergent to kill all the germs. Remember to never clean your turtle's habitat in the kitchen or bathroom sink. Even if you scrub the sink afterward, you still risk *Salmonella* infections in the sinks where you wash your dishes, clean your food, and brush your teeth!

Glossary

appetite—A desire to eat food.

bacteria—A microscopic organism.

captivity—In animals, the condition of being bred or raised by humans away from the animals' wild habitat.

carapace—The upper shell of a turtle.

carnivore—An animal that eats only meat.

cold-blooded—A condition in animals that leaves them unable to regulate their own body temperatures. Cold-blooded animals must get their heat—or cool down—through the environment. All reptiles are cold-blooded.

fossils—The hardened remains or traces of animals or plants that lived many thousands or millions of years ago.

herbivore—An animal that eats only plants.

hibernate—To spend the winter sleeping.

molting—The process of shedding. Reptiles shed their outer layers of skin.

nostrils—The openings of the nose used to take in or let out air.

omnivore—An animal that eats both meat and plants.

parasites—Organisms that live on or inside another organism, called the host. A parasite makes its host very sick or will eventually kill it.

plastron—The bottom shell of a turtle.

reptile—A type of cold-blooded animal with a backbone and dry, scaly skin.

Salmonella—A bacteria that lives harmlessly on reptiles' skin and may causes illness in humans. Different types of *Salmonella* can also be found on other places.

scutes—Hornlike scales or plates that cover the carapace in some types of turtles.

species—Groups or types of animals that have common characteristics.

terrarium—A container that is used as a habitat for pets.

veterinarian—A doctor trained to treat different types of animals.

Find Out More

Books

Bartlett, Patricia and Richard. *Aquatic Turtles: Sliders, Cooters, Painted, and Map Turtles.* Hauppauge, NY: Barron's Educational Series. 2003.

Bartlett, Patricia and Richard. *Turtles and Tortoises: A Complete Pet Owner's Manual.* Hauppauge, NY: Barron's Educational Series. 2006.

Coborn, John. *The Guide to Owning Turtles.* Neptune, NJ: TFH Publications. 1997.

Rebman, Renee C. *Turtles and Tortoises.* New York: Marshall Cavendish Benchmark, 2007.

Web Sites

World Chelonian Trust

http://www.chelonia.org/
The World Chelonian Trust Web site features detailed instructions on how to care for a variety of different turtle species.

American Tortoise Rescue

http://www.tortoise.com/
American Tortoise Rescue is an organization that takes sick or abandoned turtles and makes sure they are healthy before adopting them out to good homes. Their Web site also offers pet advice and news articles about turtles.

California Turtle & Tortoise Club

http://www.tortoise.org/cttclink.html
This Web site provides links to turtle and tortoise clubs across the United States.

Association of Reptilian and Amphibian Veterinarians

http://www.arav.org/
The ARAV can help you find a vet in your area that treats turtles.

About the Author

Johannah Haney is a freelance writer living in Boston, Massachusetts with her husband, Andrés, and their two pets. When she visits sunny Florida, she often sees wild turtles sunning themselves beside a pond outside her parents' house.

Index

Page numbers for illustrations are in **bold**.

age, 7, 9, 19

babies, **10**
box turtles, 20–21, **20**, **29**
breeders, 11, 15
breeds, 20–25

cleaning, 35–36
cold-blooded, 18, **18**
cooters, 24, **24**

endangered, 13, **17**

food, 15, 20–25, 30, 36–38, **37**, 43
fossil, **4**, 43

Galapagos, 18, 19, **19**

habitat, 12, 15, 24, 25, 32–36, **32**, **33**, **35**
        See also terrarium
heat, 18, 35
holding, 41–43, **42**

land turtles, 5, 18, 19
laws, 12
legends see mythology
light, 20, 21, 24, 34

mud turtles, 22–23, **22**
musk turtles, 22
mythology, 6, **6**, 7

painted turtles, 23–24, **23**
pet stores, 11

red-eared sliders, 18, 21, **21**
reptiles, 8, 18

sea turtles, **4**, 5, **16**, 17
shell, 23, 25, 27, 28, **28**, 29, 39, **39**
sickness, 12, 39–40, 43
size, 11, 12, 13, 18, 20–25
skin, 31, 36, 40
snappers, 14, **14**
stories, 7, **7**
swimming, 5, **14**, 24, **24**, 30

terrapin, 8, 13, **13**
terrarium, 21, **26**, 33–36, **35**
tortoise, 7, **7**, 8, 9, 18, **18**, 19, **19**
training, 38

veterinarian, 11, 25, 29, 38–39

water, 18, 20, 21, 22, 23, 24, 33, **33**, 35
Web sites, 46–47
wild turtles, 11, 12, 13, **13**